LIES

C. K. Williams

Houghton Mifflin Company

Boston   1969

Some of the poems in this collection have appeared in the follow-
ing periodicals: Carleton Miscellany: "Hood." Colorado State
Review: "Trappers," "Of What Is Past," "What Is and Is Not."
December: "In There," "Faint Praise," "Penance," "Halves," "For
Gail, When I Was Five," "Dimensions," "The Long Naked Walk
of the Dead," "It Is This Way with Men," "Sky, Water," "Being
Alone." The New Yorker: The poems "The World's Greatest Tri-
cycle-Rider" and "On the Roof" first appeared in The New Yorker.
North American Review: "The Man Who Owns Sleep," "The
Other Side," "Saint Sex." Poetry: "Sleeping Over." Stylus: "Shells."
"A Day for Anne Frank" was published by Eugene Feldman at
the Falcon Press, in Philadelphia, Pennsylvania.

LIES

for Sally

CONTENTS

LIES

BEFORE THIS

we got rid of the big people
finally we took grandpa and put half
on the mack truck and half on
the bottom grandma
we locked in with her watches
mommy and daddy had to be cut apart but they
are in separate icebergs you can't
see them under
the red lid

one place or another they are all gone
and it is hard to remember
cars? furcoats? the office?
now all there are
are roomfuls of children sleeping as far
as you can see little mattresses and
between them socks balled up and
underwear and scuffed shoes
with their mouths open

but how am I here? I feel
my lips move I count breaths I hear somebody
cry out MOTHER HELP ME somebody's hand
touches me peacefully across boundaries
kiss? hit? die? the blankets
harden with urine the fuzz
thins holes come
HOW AM I HERE? MOTHER
HOW AM I HERE?

EVEN IF I COULD

Except for the little girl
making faces behind me, and the rainbow
behind her, and the school and the truck,
the only thing between you
and infinity
is me. Which is why you cover your ears
when I speak and why
you're always oozing around the edges,
clinging, trying
to go by me.

And except for my eyes and the back
of my skull, and then my hair,
the wall, the concrete
and the fire-cloud, except for them
you would see
God. And that's why rage howls in your arms
like a baby and why I can't move —
because of the thunder and the shadows
merging like oil and the smile gleaming
through the petals.

Let me tell you how sick with loneliness
I am. What can I do while the distance
throbs on my back like a hump?
Or say, with stars stinging me
through the wheel? You are before me,
behind me things rattle their deaths out
like paper. The angels ride
in their soft saddles:
except for them, I would come closer
and go.

SAINT SEX

there are people whose sex
keeps growing even when they're old whose
genitals swell like tumors endlessly
until they are all sex and nothing else nothing
that moves or thinks nothing
but great inward and outward handfuls of gristle

think of them men
who ooze their penises out like snail
feet whose testicles clang in their scrotums women
are like anvils to them the world an
anvil they want to take whole buildings
in their arms they want
to come in the windows to run antennas
through their ducts like ramrods and women
these poor women who dream and dream of
the flower they can't sniff it sends buds
into their brain they feel their neural
river clot with moist fingers the ganglia
hardening like ant eggs the ends
burning off

pity them these people there are no wars
for them there is no news no
summer no reason they are so humble they want
nothing they have no hands or faces
pity them at night whispering I love
you to themselves and during the day how they
walk along smiling and suffering pity
them love them they are
angels

3

THE LONG NAKED WALK OF THE DEAD

for Reds

As long as they trample the sad smiles of guitars
the world won't burn. The mother speaks to her daughter
and explains: it is the breath of money in the trees
that drives angels; it is the stillness from morning
to morning when the horses of life have fallen
under their traces in the street and shudder and vanish.

It is the man who meets no one who will touch us
with sharp hands that shake over the concrete
like branches. Or the songs muttering on the paths
crisscrossing the grasses. A bench leaning back.
The sweet arms of gardeners. An enemy passing
with sons and grandsons, all just soldiers.

In flesh that only moves and speaks, the players
slide out like empty trailers to the temple country.
Six hundred thousand on the mountain when it opened.
Every word of the scream, six hundred thousand faces.
The dark metal man gleaming in the talons of silence.
Halfway down in the house of suffering, it is starting.

IN THERE

Here I am, walking along your eyelid again
toward your tear duct. Here are your eyelashes
like elephant grass and one tear
blocking the way like a boulder.

It probably takes me a long time
to figure it out, chatting with the neighbors,
trying penicillin, steam baths, meditation
on the Shekinah and sonnet cycles

and then six more months blasting
with my jackhammer before I get in there
and can wander through your face, meeting you
on the sly, kissing you from this side.

I am your own personal verb now. Here I come,
"dancing," "loving," "making cookies."
I find a telescope
and an old astronomer

to study my own face with,
and then, well, I am dreaming behind your cheekbone
about Bolivia and tangerines and the country
and here I come again, along your eyelid, walking.

LOSS

In this day and age Lord
you are like one of those poor farmers
who burns the forests off
and murders his land and then
can't leave and goes sullen and lean
among the rusting yard junk, the scrub
and the famished stock.

Lord I have felt myself raked
into the earth like manure,
harrowed and plowed under,
but I am still enough like you
to stand on the porch
chewing a stalk or drinking
while tall weeds come up dead
and the house dogs, snapping
their chains like moths, howl
and point towards the withering
meadows at nothing.

THE HARD PART

Do you remember when we dreamed about the owl
and the skeleton, and the shoe
opened and there was the angel
with his finger in the book, his smile like chocolate?

And remember? Everything that had been crushed
or burned, we changed back.
We turned the heart around
in the beginning, we closed the blossom, we let the
    drum go.

But you're missing now. Every night I feel us crying
together, but it's late —
the white bear and the lawyer
are locking the house up and where are you?

The wind walking, the rock turning over with worms
stuck to its haunches —
how will I know what loves me now
and what doesn't? How will I forgive you?

THE WORLD'S GREATEST TRICYCLE-RIDER

The world's greatest tricycle-rider
is in my heart, riding like a wildman,
no hands, almost upside down along
the walls and over the high curbs
and stoops, his bell rapid firing,
the sun spinning in his spokes like a flame.

But he is growing older. His feet
overshoot the pedals. His teeth set
too hard against the jolts, and I am afraid
that what I've kept from him is what
tightens his fingers on the rubber grips
and drives him again and again on the same block.

THE SORROW

with huge jowls that wobble with sad o
horribly sad eyes with bristles with
clothes torn tie a rag hands trembling this
burnt man in my arms won't listen he
struggles pulls loose and is going
and I am crying again Poppa Poppa it's me Poppa
but it's not it's not me I am not
someone who with these long years will
so easily retreat I am not someone after
these torments who simply cries so
I am not so unquestionably a son or
even daughter or have I face or voice
bear with me perhaps it was I who
went away perhaps I did dream it and give
birth again it doesn't matter now I stay
in my truck now I am loaded with
fruit with cold bottles with documents
of arrest and execution Father do you
remember me? how I hid and cried to you?
how my lovely genitals were bound up?
I am too small again my voice thins my
small wrists won't hold the weight again
what is forgiven? am I forgiven again?

THE MAN WHO OWNS SLEEP

The man who owns sleep
is watching the prisoners being beaten
behind the fence.
His eye pressed to the knothole,
he sees the leather curling into smiles
and snapping, he sees the intricate geography
of ruined backs,
the faces propped
open like suitcases
in the sunlight.

Who is this man
who's cornered the market
on sleeping?
He is not quite finished yet.
He bends over with a hand on his knee
to balance him
and from the other side they see
that clear eye in the wall
watching unblinking.
They see it has slept,

prisoners and guards: it drives them
to frenzies. The whips hiccup
and shriek. Those dead already roll over
and rub their retinas into the pebbles.
The man who owns sleep has had it.
He is tired.
Taking an ice cream cone
from the little wagon
he yawns and licks it.
Walking away, he yawns, licking it.

DIMENSIONS

There is a world somewhere else that is unendurable.
Those who live in it are helpless in the hands of elements,
they are like branches in the deep woods in wind
that whip their leaves off and slice the heart of the night
and sob. They are like boats bleating wearily in fog.

But here, no matter what, we know where we stand.
We know more or less what comes next. We hold out.
Sometimes a dream will shake us like little dogs, a fever
hang on so we're not ourselves or love wring us out,
but we prevail, we certify and make sure, we go on.

There is a world that uses its soldiers and widows
for flour, its orphans for building stone, its legs for pens.
In that place, eyes are softened and harmless like God's
and all blend in the traffic of their tragedy and pass by
like people. And sometimes one of us, losing the way,
will drift over the border and see them there, dying,
laughing, being revived. When we come home, we are half
    way.
Our screams heal the torn silence. We are like scars.

TO MARKET

suppose I move a factory
in here in my head in my
breast in my left hand I'm moving
dark machines in with gear boxes
and floaters and steel cams
that turn over and start things
I'm moving in fibers through
my left nostril and trucks
under my nipples and the union
has its bathroom where I think
and the stockbroker his desk
where I love

and then if I started turning
out goods and opening
shops with glass counters and rugs
what if I said
to you this is how men live and I
want to would you believe me
and love me I have my little
lunch box and my thermos and
I walk along like one leg
on the way to work swearing
I love you and we have lunch
behind the boiler and I promise
I love you and meanwhile the oil
flowing switches steam wrenches
metal I love
you and things finish get shined
up packed in streamers
mailed and I love you

12

meanwhile all this while I love
you and I'm being bought pieces
of me at five dollars
and parts at ten cents and
here I am still saying I love
you under the stacks under
the windows with wires the smoke
going up I love
you I love you

WHAT IS AND IS NOT

I am a long way from that place,
but I can still hear
the impatient stamp of its hoof
near the fire, and the green clicking
of its voices and its body flowing.

At my window, the usual spirits,
the same silence. A child would see it
as my clothes hanging like killers
on the door, but I don't, and it
doesn't creak in the hallway for me.

It is not death. In your face
I glimpse it. You are reaching
a hand out comfortingly
though it snarls, plunges,
and you know that the baby

will not look up from its game
of beauty. It is not love or hate
or passion. It does not touch us,
dream us, speak, sing or
come closer, yet we consume it.

HOOD

Remember me? I was the one
in high school you were always afraid of.
I kept cigarettes in my sleeve, wore
engineer's boots, long hair, my collar
up in back and there were always
girls with me in the hallways.

You were nothing. I had it in for you —
when I peeled rubber at the lights
you cringed like a teacher.
And when I crashed and broke both lungs
on the wheel, you were so relieved
that you stroked the hard Ford paint
like a breast and your hands shook.

TWICE MORE

understand me please there's no man underneath there's
no woman no dog no opening what happens in the first
place is hunger is silence a cold
mathematical thumb-mark and
everytime I hurt I didn't mean it
and when the shame quit closing its little mouth locking
its feet down melting what happened
was that they didn't care they ticked
a night off they counted
me up they threw my name back

so understand me the long emblem of death is **wa**shed out
the famous scar cries but
if I wanted you I still would if I desired
I would if I cut the mistake down
there is a man with nothing in
him but blood there is a blank
gene drifting a bone with cells
in it and I am myself again I start
again I walk
in a storm of lost handfuls and tell them
and twice more I tell them and
twice more
I am myself again

ON THE ROOF

The trouble with me is that whether I get love or not
I suffer from it. My heart always seems to be prowling
a mile ahead of me, and, by the time I get there to surround
    it,
it's chewing fences in the next county, clawing
the bank-vault wall down or smashing in the window
I'd just started etching my name on with my diamond.

And that's how come I end up on the roof. Because even if
    I talk
into my fist everyone still hears my voice like the ocean
in theirs, and so they solace me and I have to keep
breaking toes with my gun-boots and coming up here
to live — by myself, like an aerial, with a hand on the ledge,
one eye glued to the tin door and one to the skylight.

IT IS THIS WAY WITH MEN

They are pounded into the earth
like nails; move an inch,
they are driven down again.
The earth is sore with them.
It is a spiny fruit
that has lost hope
of being raised and eaten.
It can only ripen and ripen.
And men, they too are wounded.
They too are sifted from their loss
and are without hope. The core
softens. The pure flesh softens
and melts. There are thorns, there
are the dark seeds, and they end.

SLEEPING OVER

for Dave and Mark

There hasn't been any rain
since I arrived. The lawns
are bleached and tonight goldenrod
and burnt grass reflect
across my walls like ponds.
After all these days
the textures and scents of my room
are still strange and comforting.
The pines outside, immobile
as chessmen, fume turps
that blend with the soap taste
of the sheets and with the rot
of camphor and old newspapers
in the bare bureau drawers.
Jarred by a headlight's glare
from the country road, the crumbling
plaster swarms with shadows.
The bulb in the barn, dull
and eternal, sways and flickers
as though its long drool
of cobwebs had been touched,
and the house loosens, unmoors,
and, distending and shuddering, rocks
me until I fall asleep.

In december the mare
I learned to ride on died.
On the frozen paddock hill,
down, she moaned all night

before the mink farmers
came in their pickup
truck, sat on her dark
head and cut her throat.
I dream winter. Shutters
slamming apart. Bags
crammed with beer bottles
tipping against clapboard.
Owls in chimneys.
Drafts; thieves; snow.
Over the crusty fields
scraps of blue loveletters
mill wildly like children,
and a fat woman, her rough
stockings tattered away
at a knee, sprints in high,
lumbering bounds among
the skating papers. Out
to the road — red hydrant,
bus bench, asphalt —
a wasp twirling at her feet,
she is running back.

My first kiss was here.
I can remember the spot —
next to a path, to
a cabin, to a garden patch —
but not how it happened
or what I felt, except
amazement that a kiss
could be soundless. Now,
propped up on an elbow,
I smoke through the dawn, smudging
the gritty sheets with ashes,

wondering what if that night
someone nearby had snorted
aloud, had groaned or even
just rustled a branch.

Day finally. The trees
and fences clarify, unsnarl.
Flagstones, coins, splash
across the driveway crowns
and the stark underbrush
animals go away.
A rickety screendoor bangs,
slaps its own echo
twice. There are no footsteps
but someone is out sifting
ashes in the garbage pit.
Suddenly dishes jangle
the bright middle distances
and the heat begins again:
by now the ground must be
hard and untillable as ice.
Far off from the house,
the lake, jellied with umber
weed scum, tilts toward
the light like a tin tray.
Dead rowboats clog
the parched timber dam
and along the low banks
the mounds of water rubble
I gathered yesterday
have dried and shrunk down
to a weak path wobbling
back and forth from the edge.

THREE SEASONS AND A GORILLA

these americans just looking
you can tell their big toenails are
blue with welts running
across the base and pain
you can tell the pain miles
from here you can smell
it
and these frenchmen jesus
infections on
the hairline and what pain you need
the wind
but o god what wailing from each
follicle each
strand

and these asians
and these southamericans and
eskimos
think of the clogged pores
in the armpit and the
raw spots at the root
of the penis and the pimple that grows
inwards and shoots and
again again what
agony what cold misery coming
back hitting you in the neck what
stinking and take me
a big clothes-
bag the buttons
all crying the zippers

giving up the seams the torn
crotch lines groaning and just
think what pain god what
pain

THE OTHER SIDE

Across the way hands
move nervously on curtains,
and behind them, radiated
with arc-vapor light, silver,
there is almost no face.
Almost no eyes look at me through this air.
Almost no mouth twists
and repeats, following my mouth, the shrill ciphers
that cross like swallows.

Tonight the breeze from the distillery
stinks of death. Do you think men have died
in the vats tonight? Everyone waits,
sick with the stench of mash
and spirits, and the tubs lick
their own sides with little splashes,
little bubbles that pop, clearing themselves.

In this breeze, it is strange to be telling myself,
Life, what are you saying?
In this breeze, almost like hands, words
climb on the thin gauze of curtains
and drop off. Men float
from corner to corner, and, almost like hands,
birds put their sore wings under the eaves
and sleep.

OF WHAT IS PAST

I hook my fingers into the old tennis court fence
and kneel down in an overgrowth of sharp weeds
to watch the troopers in their spare compound drill.

Do you remember when this was a park? When girls
swung their rackets here in the hot summer mornings
and came at night to open their bodies to us?

Now gun-butts stamp the pale clay like hooves.
Hard boots gleam.
And still, children play tag and hide-and-seek

beyond the barriers. Lovers sag in the brush.
It is not them, it is us: we know too much.
Soon only the past will know what we know.

ASHES ASHES WE ALL FALL DOWN

how come when grandpa is teaching the little boy
to sing he can't no matter what remember even
though he taps time hard with his teeth like a cricket even
though he digs in hard with his fingers how come?

and when he grows tall he will name everyone
he meets father or mother but will still have no songs
he leans back among the cold pages he falls down
in the palace of no sleep where the king cries and

in the new country the musical soldiers will
beat him he will sell silver consonants out
of his car the lady will cup his dry testicles
in the drone the soldiers beat him again

I miss you now can you
remember the words at least? and the
new name? when pain comes
you must kill it when beauty comes

with her smiles you must kill them I
miss you again I miss you white
bug I miss you sorrow rain radio I miss
you old woman in my bible in the dream

TRAPPERS

In the dark with an old song
I sit, in the silence,
and it knows me
by heart and comes faltering
gently through me
like a girl in love,
in a room, evening,
feeling her way.

When good mountain men
were snowed in in the Rockies
for months and months, sleet
hissing over the sharp crust
to hollow places, branches
groaning through the night,
they must have done what I do
now, and been as terrified.

I let a word out,
and what comes, an awful drone,
a scab, bubbles up
and drills away unfadingly.
Later, in a place far
from here, feeling softly on her neck
like a fly, she will gaze
into the sunlight, and not see me.

BEING ALONE

Never on one single pore Eternity
have I been touched by your snows

or felt your shy mouth tremble,
your breath break on me

like the white wave. I have not felt
your nakedness tear me

with hunger or your silver hands
betray me but today I promise

whatever flower of your house
should bloom I will stay

locked to its breast.
Like little fish who live

harmlessly under the bellies of sharks,
I will go where you go,

drift inconspicuously
in the raw dredge of your power

like a leaf, a bubble of carrion,
a man who has understood and does not.

TRASH

I am your garbage man. What you leave,
I keep for myself, burn or throw
on the dump or from scows in the delicious river.
Your old brown underpants are mine now,
I can tell from them
what your dreams were. I remember
how once in a closet with shoes
whispering and mothballs, you held on
and cried like a woman. Your nights stink
of putrid lampshades, of inkwells and silk
because my men and I with our trails
of urine and soft eggs and our long brooms
hissing, came close.

What do they do with kidneys and toes
in hospitals? And where did your old dog go
who peed on the rug and growled?
They are in my house now, and what grinds
in your wife's teeth while she sleeps,
that is mine. She is chewing
on embryos, on the eyes of your lover,
on your phone book and the empty glass
you left in the kitchen. And in your body,
the one who died there and rots
secretly in the fingers of your spirit,
she is hauling his genitals out, basket
after basket
and mangling all of it in the crusher.

GIVING IT UP

It is an age
of such bestial death
that even before we die
our ghosts go.
I have felt mine while I slept
send shoots over my face,
probing some future char
there, tasting the flesh
and the sweat
as though for the last time.

And I have felt him
extricate himself and go,
crying, softening himself
and matching his shape
to new bodies; merging,
sliding into souls,
into motors, buildings,
stop signs, policemen —
anything.

By morning, he is back.
Diminished, shorn
of his light, he lies crumpled
in my palm, shivering
under my breath like cellophane.
And every day
there is nothing to do
but swallow him like a cold
tear
and get on with it.

FOR GAIL, WHEN I WAS FIVE

My soul is out back eating your soul.
I have you tied in threads like a spider
and I am drinking down your laughter
in huge spoonfuls. It is like tinsel.
It sprays over the crusty peach baskets
and the spades hung on pegs. It is like air
and you are screaming, or I am, and we are
in different places with wild animal faces.

What does God do to children who touch
in the darkness of their bodies and laugh?
What does he think of little underpants
that drift down on the hose like flowers?
God eats your soul, like me. He drinks
your laughter. It is God in the history
of my body who melts your laughter
and spits it in the wounds of my life like tears.

DON'T

I have been saying what I have to say
for years now, backwards and forwards
and upside-down and you haven't heard
it yet, so from now on
I'm going to start unsaying it:
I'm going to unsay what I've said already
and what everyone else has said
and what hasn't even been said yet.

I'm going to unsay
the northern hemisphere
and the southern,
east and west, up
and down, the good
and the bad. I'm going to unsay
what floats just over my skin
and just under: the leaves
and the roots, the worm
in the river and the whole river
and the ocean and the ocean
under the ocean. Space
and light are going,
silence, sound, flags,
photographs, dollar bills:
the sewer people and the junk people,
the money people and the concrete people
who ride out of town on dreams
and love it, and the dreams,
even the one pounding
under the floor like a drum —
I'm going to run them all down

32

again the other way
and end at the bottom.

Do you see? Caesar is unsaid
now. Christ
is unsaid. They trade toys
but it's too late.
The doctor is unsaid, cured;
the rubber sheet grows
leaves, luscious and dark,
and the patient feels them
gathering at the base
of his spine like a tail.
It is unsaid
that we have no tails —
an old lady twirls hers
and lifts
like a helicopter.

Time turns
backwards in its womb and floats out
in its unsaying.
It won't start again.
The sad physicist
throws switches but all
the bomb does is sigh inwardly
and hatch like an egg,
and little void-creatures
come, who live
in the tones between notes,
innocent and unstruck.

A baby fighting for air

through her mother's breast
won't anymore: the air is unsaid.
The skeleton I lost in France
won't matter. No picnics,
no flattened grass,
no bulls.

Everything washes up,
clean as morning.
My wife's wet underwear in the sink —
I unsay them,
they swallow me
like a Valentine.
The icebox is growing baby green
lima beans for Malcolm Lowry.
The house fills with love.
I chew perfume
and my neighbor kissing me good morning
melts and goes out
like a light.

There is bare rock
between here and the end.
There is a burnt place
in the silence.

Along my ribs, dying of old age,
the last atom dances
like a little girl. I unsay
her yellow dress, her hair,
her slippers
but she keeps dancing,
jumping back and forth

from my face to my funny bone
until I burst out laughing.

And then I unsay
the end.

JUST RIGHT

the way we get under cars and in
motors you'd think we were made for them our hands
slotting in the carbs our feet
on the pedals and how everything
even flowers even the horns of cattle fits
just right it is like nail and hole
even apples even hand-grenades with indentations
for our fingers and the detonations patterns finding us
all this given and how ungrateful we are
dreaming that someday we won't touch anything
that all this space will close on us
the fire sprout through us and blossom and
the tides

dear father of the fire save me enough room please
and dear water-mother I'd like two clear drops
to float in brothers and sisters I'll need
your engines and computers I'll need four tall buildings
and heaters and strong-bulldozers with
thick threads and switches and there must be
uniforms
there must be maps and hoses and
tiled rooms to drain the blood off
and will your voices
come telling me you love me? and your mouths
and hands? and your cold
music? every inch of me? every
hour of me?

AFTER THAT

Do you know how much pain is left
in the world? One tiny bit of pain is left,
braised on one cell like a toothmark.
And how many sorrows there still are? Three sorrows:
the last, the next to the last and this one.

And there is one promise left, feeling
its way through the poison, and one house
and one gun and one shout of agony
that wanders in the lost cities and the lost mountains.
And so this morning, suffering the third sorrow

from the last, feeling pain in my last gene,
cracks in the struts, bubbles in the nitro,
this morning for someone I'm not even sure exists
I waste tears. I count down by fractions
through the ash. I howl. I use up everything.

OR

Here's where I started
running from a little bee
is here now coated with soot his back legs
stuck together with black honey
black granules
on his jaws he speaks in my voice
he spreads his wings and something
budges in him but
not me

I'm here now

I found one day
without dying

I found it when everyone
except for one man
cursing kept
quiet everyone but one corpse
with gold

in its gullet

I found it when
when I said HANDS
I meant
your breasts when I said
SILENCE I meant
what never
touches

And did I come back?

I'm in eight pieces
like a toy truck
I'm in the mailbox I'm
in the cabin by the pond
I'm on the lawn

am I still
running?

I'm still running I'm still holding
everything together I'm still
me

I got there
where the lines met where
the laughter
opened the stones
desired something the slash mark
cried I got
there I got back I'm still
running nothing
comes in nothing
goes out I
see

TEN BELOW

It is bad enough crying for children
suffering neglect and starvation in our world
without having on a day like this
to see an old cart-horse covered with foam,
quivering so hard that when he stops
the wheels still rock slowly in place
like gears in an engine.
A man will do that, shiver where he stands,
frozen with false starts
before decisions, just staring,
but with a man you can take his arm,
talk him out of it, lead him away.

What do you do when both hands
and your voice are simply goads?
When the eyes you solace see space,
the wall behind you, the wisp of grass
pushing up through the curb at your feet?
I have thought that all the animals
we kill and maim, if they wanted to
could stare us down, wither us
and turn us into smoke with their glances —
they forbear because they pity us,
like angels, and love of something else
is why they suffer us and submit.

But this is Pine Street, Philadelphia, 1965.
You don't believe
in anything divine being here.
There is an old plug with a worn blanket
thrown on its haunches. There is a wagon

full of junk — pipes and rotted sinks,
the grates from furnaces — and there
is a child walking beside the horse
with sugar, and the mammoth head lowering,
delicately nibbling from those vulnerable
fingers. You can't cut your heart out.
Sometimes, just what is, is enough.

TAILS

there was this lady once she used to grow
snakes in her lap

they came up like tulips
from her underpants and the tops
of her stockings and she'd get us
with candy and have us pet
the damned things

god they were horrible skinned
snakes all dead
it turned out she'd catch
them in the garden and skin
them and drive
knitting needles up along the spines
and sew them on
it stank
the skins rotting in the corner heads
scattered all over the floor

it turned out she loved
children she wanted
to do something
for us we ate
the candy of course we touched
the snakes we
hung around god
we hated her she was
terrible

SKY, WATER

for Bruce and Fox

They can be fists punching the water —
muskrats, their whole bodies plunging
through weak reeds from the bank,
or the heads of black and white ducks
that usually flicker in quietly
and come up pointing heavenwards.

A man can lie off the brown scum of a slough
and watch how they will go in like blades,
deeply, to the bottom,
and in his pale silence
with the long field furrows strumming
like distant music,
he will wonder at and pity
the creatures hooked together like flowers on the water,
who will die flashing in the air,
shaken in the beak of sunlight.

The surface tainted with small blood,
there can be bees and water hydra,
sea-grasses and blown seed,
and before a man's eyes life and death,
silence and the dim scream of love
can rise and furl up
from the bottom like smoke
and thin away.

OUT HERE

here is a man eating
a woman he is on the bones
now the grinder blades crack
off pieces he makes
soups ribs floating like feathers
dark froggy vertebrae
squatting
on the bottom

am I? I look so much
like you now that
no one tells me anything
no one even loves me
unless I cry no one
comes except to lift
me and rub me against
them or believes me

but they are very
kind I am warmer and also
darling I am wearing
your skirts
and your shoes they have given me
your long hair do you remember
how lovely we were how my kiss
hung in the clear silence?

don't be afraid I'm not
angry now I'm not lonely
I swear this is my last
breast I do not desire you I

44

sip with my own rose now
this evening wanting you I
have money the brown wall the
signs I'm not selfish

DOWNWARDS

This is the last day of the world. On the river docks
I watch for the last time the tide get higher
and chop in under the stinking pilings. How the small
    creatures
who drift dreaming of hands and lungs must sting,
rotting alive in the waste spill, coming up dead
with puffy stomachs paler than the sky or faces.
There is deep fire fuming ash to the surface.
It is the last tide and the last evening and from now
things will strive back downwards.
A fish thrown up will gasp in the flare
and flop back hopelessly through the mud flats to the
    water.
The last man, an empty bottle with no message, is here,
    is me,
and I am rolling, fragile as a bubble in the upstream
    spin,
battered by carcasses, drawn down by the lips of weeds
to the terrible womb of torn tires and children's plastic
    shoes
and pennies and urine. I am no more, and what is left,
softly baled with wire, floating
like a dark pillow in the hold of the brown ship, it is
    nothing.
It dreams. Touching fangs delicately with cranes
and forklifts, it rests silently in its heavy ripening.
It stands still on the water, rocking, blinking.

SHELLS

It's horrible, being run over by a bus
when all you are is a little box turtle.
You burst. Your head blasts out like a cork
and soars miles
to where the boy sprawls on the grass strip
beside the sidewalk. In mid-air
you are him. Your face touches his face,
you stutter, and you will go all your life
holding your breath,
wondering what you meant.

                           He forgets now
but he knew it in his cheek scorched
by the sweet blades and in his wild groin.
In his mother's arms, screaming,
he knew it: that he was crossing
under the laughter and there was the other voice
sobbing, It's not far, It's not far.

BEYOND

Some people,
they just don't hate enough yet.
They back up, snarl, grab guns
but they're like children,
they overreach themselves;
they end up standing there feeling stupid,
wondering if it's worth it.

Some people, they don't have a cause yet.
They just throw their hate here and there
and sooner or later it's hollow
and they say, What is this?
and after that it's too late.
After that you can barely
button your sleeve in the morning —
you just take breaths.

Some people are too tired to hate
and so they think, Why live?
They read the papers, wince,
but they're hardly there anymore.
You go by them in the street
and they don't spit or mutter —
they look at themselves in store windows,
they touch their faces.

Some people, you give up
on them. You let them go,
you lose them.
They were like children, they hardly
knew what they meant. You think to yourself,
Good Riddance.

SATURDAY

I hate reading about dead men knowing
that in the end they cut him down
anyway and he went out screaming
for his wife in tears and I hate it also
about all the poor murderers in jail on their
birthdays what do they think about the rain
streaming the double doors the toilet
in the corner maybe they're sensitive they
want you to shit while they're asleep please
maybe they don't ever want to get up again
and people who are so proud
of their teeth they have mirrors over the bed
and a loudspeaker and they listen to them
clack clack all day what about them
he's thinking about ten thousand men
their arms over their heads their dirty
skirts flying all running at him turbans
sandals loose on the ground hands flapping
they have mustaches most
of them beards beautiful wrists and then
he thinks it's my birthday too and he goes
clack again clack clack and says
please not now it's raining my birthday
please one more day I hate this
the way he just shivers and doesn't do
anything the way the rain just keeps coming
the walls just
stand there
from now on I'm not saying it I'm going
to be saturday from now on and not
touch it there is a white flower there
is a postmark that's all

49

PATIENCE IS WHEN YOU STOP WAITING

I stand on the first step under the torn mouths of hours
in a new suit. Terrified of the arched webs and the dust,
of my speech, my own hair slicked with its thin pride,
I jut like a thorn; I turn, my pain turns and closes.

Tell me again about silence. Tell me I won't,
not ever, hear the cold men whispering in my pores
or the mothers and fathers who scream in the bedroom
and throw boxes of money between them and kiss.

At the window, faces hover against the soft glow
like names. If I cry out, it will forget me and go;
if I don't, nothing begins again. Tell me
about mercy again, how she rides in eternity's arms

in the drifts and the dreams come. The night is dying.
Wisely it thinks of death as a thing born of desire.
Gently it opens its sharp ribs and bites through
and holds me. Tell me about my life again, where it is now.

FAINT PRAISE

for Jim Moss, 1935–1961

Whatever last slump of flesh
rolls like a tongue in the mouth of your grave,
whatever thin rags of your underwear
are melting in slow, tiny stomachs,
I am still here; I have survived.

I thought when you died that your angels,
stern, dangerous bats with their cameras and laws,
would swarm like bees
and that the silences flaming from you
would fuse me like stone.

There were no new landscapes I could prepare for you.
I let you go.
And tonight, again, I will eat, read,
and my wife and I will move into love
in the swells of each other like ships.
The loose aerial outside will snap,
the traffic lights blink and change,
the dried lives of autumn crackle like cellophane.

And I will have my life still.
In the darkness, it will lie over against me,
it will whisper, and somehow,
after everything, open to me again.

HALVES

I am going to rip myself down the middle into two pieces
because there is something in me that is neither
the right half nor the left half nor between them.
It is what I see when I close my eyes, and what I see.

As in this room there is something neither ceiling
nor floor, not space, light, heat or even
the deep skies of pictures, but something that beats softly
against others when they're here and others not here,

that leans on me like a woman,
curls up in my lap and walks
with me to the kitchen or out of the house altogether
to the street — I don't feel it, but it beats and beats;

so my life: there is this, neither before me
nor after, not up, down, backwards nor forwards from me.
It is like the dense, sensory petals in a breast
that sway and touch back. It is like the mouth of a season,

the cool speculations bricks murmur, the shriek in orange,
and though it is neither true nor false, it tells me
that it is quietly here, and, like a creature, is in pain;
that when I ripen it will crack open the locks, it will love
   me.

PENANCE

I only regret the days wasted in no pain.
I am sorry for having touched bottom
and loved again.
I am sorry for the torn sidewalks
and the ecstacy underneath, for the cars,
the old flower-lady watching her fingers,
my one shoe in the morning
with death on its tongue.

In the next yard a dog whines
and whines for his lost master
and for the children who have gone
without him. I am sorry
because his teeth click on my neck,
because my chest shudders and the owl cries
in the tug of its fierce sacrament.

I repent God and children,
the white talons of peace and my jubilance.
Everything wheels
in the iron rain, smiling and lying.
Forgive me, please.

IT IS TEEMING

In rain like this what you want is an open barn door
to look out from. You want to see the deep hoofprints
in the yard fill and overflow, to smell the hay and hear
the stock chewing and stamping and their droppings pat-
    tering.

Of course the messengers would come away. A wet
    mutt,
his underlip still crisp with last night's chickenblood
will drift through the gate and whine and nuzzle
your knee with a bad look like a secret drinker,

and you will wish for the lions, the claws that erected
and slashed back, because you are tired of lording it,
of caving ribs in, of swinging axes and firing.
Where are the angels with trucks who pulled the trees
    down?

Now it is pure muck, half cow-shit, half mud and blood,
    seething.
You have to go out back, dragging it, of course. No one
sees you with it. The rain — you throw wakes up like a
    giant.
The way you wanted it, the way it would be, of course.

FROM NOW ON

for Murray Dessner

this knowledge so innocently it goes this sin
it dies without looking back it ripens
and dissolves and behind it behind
january behind bread and trenches there
are rooms with no gods in them there are breasts
with no deaths anymore and no promises
I knew mercy would leave me and turn
back I knew things in their small nests would
want me and say Come and things blossoming
say Go Downwards but still am I no bigger
than one man? not a pint more? a
watt? a filament of pity or sweetness? I turn
over first one side heads and then tails
I love life first then death first I
close I open I split down like an amoeba
into bricks and sunrise and longing
but we are suffering seven directions at once
the mouths in our mouths don't tell us
the sorrowful faces in our tears not
touch us nothing holds us nothing reaps
us we are not lived we are not suffered
the dreams come for us but they fail

OUR GREY

it is the Toy-Eater scattering
his treasure in the cities beneath
benches beneath cars and sewer plates this
immense treasure which men harvest
and add up and so with their metal hands
the children solace the scars of
the monster in their beds and so
there is sleep and there are ashes and
the dangerous money the
finish and there are no voices no
sadnesses the Toy-Eater has crawled
to the last edge and looked in and only
the Toy-Eater now only the
treasure only our poor lives

A DAY FOR ANNE FRANK

God hates you!
> — St. John Chrysostom

1.

I look onto an alley here
where, though tough weeds and flowers thrust up
through cracks and strain
toward the dulled sunlight,
there is the usual filth spilling from cans,
the heavy soot shifting in the gutters.
People come by mostly
to walk their dogs or take the shortcut
between the roaring main streets,
or just to walk
and stare up at the smoky windows,
but this morning when I looked out
children were there running back and forth
between the houses toward me.
They were playing with turtles —
skimming them down the street
like pennies or flat stones,
and bolting, shouting, after the broken corpses.
One had a harmonica, and as he ran,
his cheeks bloating and collapsing like a heart,
I could hear its bleat, and then the girls' screams
suspended behind them with their hair,
and all of them: their hard, young breath,
their feet pounding wildly on the pavement to the corner.

2.

I thought of you at that age.
Little Sister, I thought of you,
thin as a door,
and of how your thighs would have swelled
and softened like cake,
your breasts have bleached
and the new hair growing on you like song
would have stiffened and gone dark.
There was rain for a while, and then not.
Because no one came, I slept again,
and dreamed that you were here with me,
snarled on me like wire,
tangled so closely to me that we were vines
or underbrush together,
or hands clenched.

3.

They are cutting babies in half on bets.
The beautiful sergeant has enough money to drink
for a week.
The beautiful lieutenant can't stop betting.
The little boy whimpers
he'll be good.
The beautiful cook is gathering up meat
for the dogs.
The beautiful dogs

love it all.
Their flanks glisten.
They curl up in their warm kennels
and breathe.
They breathe.

4.

Little Sister,
you are a clot
in the snow,
blackened,
a chunk of phlegm
or puke

and there are men with faces
leaning over you with watercans

watering you!
in the snow, as though flowers would sprout
from your armpits
and genitals.

Little Sister,
I am afraid of the flowers sprouting from you

I am afraid of the silver petals
that crackle
of the stems darting
in the wind
of the roots

5.

The twilight rots.
Over the greasy bridges and factories,
it dissolves
and the clouds swamp in its rose
to nothing.
I think sometimes the slag heaps by the river
should be bodies
and that the pods of moral terror
men make of their flesh should split
and foam their cold, sterile seeds into the tides
like snow
or ash.

6.

Stacks of hair were there
little mountains
the gestapo children must have played in
and made love in and loved
the way children love haystacks or mountains

O God the stink
of hair oil and dandruff

their mothers must have thrown them into their tubs
like puppies and sent them to bed

coming home so filthy stinking

of jew's hair

of gold fillings, of eyelids

7.

Under me on a roof
a sparrow little by little
is being blown away.
A cage of bone is left,
part of its wings,
a stain.

8.

And in Germany the streetcar conductors go to work
in their stiff hats,
depositing workers and housewives
where they belong,
pulling the bell chains,
moving drive levers forward or back.

9.

*I am saying good-bye to you before our death. Dear
Father: I am saying good-bye to you before my death.
We are so anxious to live, but all is lost — we are not
allowed! I am so afraid of this death, because little
children are thrown into graves alive. Good-bye
forever.*

I kiss you.

10.

Come with me Anne.
Come,
it is rotten not to be anywhere at all,

to have no one
like an old whore,
a general.

Come sit with me here
kiss me; my heart too is wounded
with forgiveness.

There is an end now.
Stay.
Your foot hooked through mine
your hand against my hand
your hip touching me lightly

it will end now
it will not begin again

Stay
they will pass
and not know us

the cold brute earth
is asleep

there is no danger

there is nothing

Anne

there is nothing